A MEMOIR

Pieces of ME

ELVA CHASE

Esquire Publications
Jacksonville, FL 32258
www.esquirepublications.com
Tel: 1-800-501-7640

"Pieces of Me"

LCCN: 2026940016
ISBN: 979-8-9900739-9-9

INTENTIONALLY LEFT BLANK

Introduction

"The Lord is close to the brokenhearted and saves those who are crushed in spirit." — Psalm 34:18

I stayed. I endured. I carried the weight of homes, hearts, and broken promises while storms raged around me. I faced abuse, physical, emotional, and psychological, from the men I loved. And yet, I never walked away from my responsibilities, from my children, from the life I built with sweat, tears, and unwavering faith.

And now… the children I gave everything to are choosing their own paths, and sometimes those paths include speaking words that hurt me deeply. Feeling unloved. Unappreciated. They judge. They accuse. They forget, in the moment, the sacrifices made in silence, the meals prepared, the nights spent awake worrying, the love given even when it was messy, unthankful, or unnoticed.

This book is my story. Each chapter carries a piece of that truth, one for each child, one for each relationship, one for each lesson learned through pain. These pages are not about anger or bitterness. They are about the hurt that comes from loving fully, and the resilience that comes from trusting God even when hearts break.

I am sharing this because I know many mothers and many people carry silent struggles. It gets heavy, and some walk away. I am sharing this because even when the world does not see your pain, God does. And in Him, we are never truly broken.

I am here. I am standing. And though they tried, they did not break me.

To My Children

You've been the greatest part of my life. Through every hardship, you were my reason to keep going. I know I wasn't perfect, but I prayed, I tried, and I loved you with everything in me—even when life felt heavy. God carried us. You are my greatest joy and most valuable gift. Wherever life leads you, remember this: You were, and always will be, the best part of my story. And God's not finished with you yet. Lord, keep guiding them. Hold their hearts close to You. In Jesus' name, Amen.

A MEMOIR
Pieces of ME
ELVA CHASE

Foreword

"He heals the brokenhearted and binds up their wounds."
— Psalm 147:3

This book is not written out of anger or revenge. It is written out of truth. Out of the quiet, unseen moments when I gave everything I had and still felt misunderstood, unseen, and even blamed.

Every mother carries a story. Every mother gives, protects, and loves, even when it goes unrecognized. I am no different. But sometimes, even the deepest love is met with disappointment, hurt, or confusion. My story is about that love and that hurt.

In sharing my journey, I hope to offer a window into the complexity of motherhood, resilience, and faith. To be honest about the pain of feeling betrayed by those we love most. To show that even when hearts break, we can remain whole with God's guidance.

This book is my testament to survival, to faith, and to the quiet strength that comes from enduring life's storms without losing yourself. It is for anyone who has loved fully and felt the sting of being misunderstood.

I invite you to walk through these chapters with me, not to assign blame, but to witness the journey of a mother who has loved, hurt, and ultimately, survived.

Chapter 1

My Children

"Even though I walk through the darkest valley, I will fear no evil, for you are with me." — Psalm 23:4

I held you close when you were small, even when life felt like it was falling apart. You may not have known it, but while you were laughing, learning, and growing, I carried burdens you could never see. I worked tirelessly to keep our lives stable, often juggling jobs, responsibilities, and the emotional weight of a heart that had been broken more than once.

I lived in the quiet struggles and sacrifices that no one noticed. There were sacrifices I never spoke about, not because they didn't matter, but because I didn't want you to carry them.

There were days and weeks I didn't eat, drinking water just to quiet the hunger, just to make sure there was enough for you. I would convince myself I wasn't hungry, telling myself I needed to lose weight and stay in shape. I would work out, not always for health, but to silence what I was going without. You never saw that part. You saw meals. You saw things come together. You saw me show up. But behind that was a mother making sure you were full, even when she wasn't.

There came a point when things got so difficult that our car was repossessed. I remember walking miles to the welfare office, tears streaming down my face, feeling a level of humiliation I had never known before. I couldn't even hide it. I walked in broken, trying to hold myself together in front of a social worker while my emotions poured out anyway. But she was kind. Gentle. Understanding in a way I needed in that moment.

I applied for food stamp assistance, something I never imagined I would have to do. And while I felt the weight of it, I was also grateful. It helped us get through a hard season.

I didn't stay there long. In less than a year, I found a second job and was able to come off assistance. But that moment stayed with me. Not just the struggle, but the reminder of how far I was willing to go…just to make sure you were okay. And I would do it all over again.

There were nights I cried silently after another failed relationship, wondering if love would ever feel safe or real. Early mornings came just as quickly, getting up for work while worrying whether there would be enough money for rent or groceries. I made decisions to protect you, even when it meant putting my own needs last, again and again.

I wrestled with my faith, straddling the line between what I believed and the fear that life had taken too much from me to trust fully. I questioned, I doubted, I stumbled, but I never stopped seeking God. That journey through uncertainty shaped me, even when it felt impossible to carry both hope and hurt at the same time.

And then there were the men I believed could be my forever, men who instead brought pain, both physical and emotional. Loving them, trusting them, and hoping for safety only to be hurt repeatedly was exhausting. Yet, I endured, not because I wanted to, but because the stakes were higher than my own comfort, you, my children, and the life we were building together.

The books I wrote about them came from lived experience, not perception. And while time may offer different versions of the past, and the relationships you now have with your dads may look different, the life we lived and the struggles we faced will always speak for themselves.

Through all of this, unhealed with no outlet, I tried to show up for you, to be present, to love you fully. I may have been tired, bruised, or uncertain, but my heart was always yours. You saw the laughter, the play, the hard times, the shaky stability, but you didn't see the nights I wrestled with fear, the moments I doubted myself, or the inner strength I had to summon just to make it through another day.

This chapter is my testament to the unseen sacrifices, the quiet endurance, and the journey from fear to faith. I write it not to assign blame or to make you feel guilty, but to honor the life I lived for you, the love I gave quietly, the struggles I bore silently, and the resilience that carried us all through the hardest times.

Life is not perfect. Neither was I. But through every challenge, every tear, every quiet, unseen battle, I survived, and so has my love for you.

Chapter 2

Before Life Taught Me Otherwise

"Train up a child in the way he should go, and when he is old, he will not depart from it." — Proverbs 22:6

I always felt like I had a good childhood. I didn't know we didn't have much, because what we had felt like enough to me. There was love, there was pain, there was laughter, and there were moments that filled my heart in ways I didn't understand until I got older.

I was quiet growing up. Introverted in many ways. But around people who made me feel comfortable, I was the complete opposite, a chatterbox, full of thoughts, laughter, and curiosity. I didn't open up easily, but when I did, it was real.

I was strong, even back then. Strong in a way that helped me push through challenges, but also in a way that made me hold on longer than I should have. I had a forgiving heart, one that didn't always know when to let go, even when people hurt me on purpose.

I spent a lot of time with my brothers and cousins. I was a tomboy. We played alley stickball, and they always made me the pitcher because they said I had "an arm." I didn't think much of it at the time, but my high school coach did. She wanted me to play for the school, but I couldn't bring myself to ask my mother for the money for uniforms and away games. I didn't want to be a burden.

I loved to draw. I was a sketch artist before I even knew what that meant. I once entered a contest by mail and drew cartoon characters, Porky Pig, Daffy Duck, and Bugs Bunny. My drawings were so good that the people from the contest actually came to our home and wanted me to join their art school in Philadelphia. Two middle-aged white men in suits. They couldn't believe my drawings came from a 12-

year-old. Things were different back then. Opportunities didn't always come with access. My mother couldn't afford it, and that was that. Still, I created. I imagined. I found joy in what I had. I later developed a love of architecture, fascinated by the structure and design of buildings. My first love.

Some of my favorite meals were the simplest ones. Mayonnaise sandwiches. Syrup sandwiches. Oscar Mayer bologna with hot sauce and pepper sandwiches. To anyone else, it might not have been much, but to me, they were the best things ever. My favorite colors were black and brown, and later in life, I discovered colors.

I attended a modeling and acting school for a while called Barbizon, one of the biggest in the country, but eventually, I told my mother I didn't feel comfortable there. I wasn't into makeup like that or prissy stuff. It didn't feel like me.

I was happiest outside, running with my brothers and cousins, playing tag football until the streetlights came on. And on some nights, as long as my brothers were with me, Mommy would let us go to the firehouse that was across the street from our home. They hung out with their friends, but I would lie on the grass and stare at the sky, loving on the stars, trying to find the Big Dipper and the Little Dipper until they said it was time to go home. One night, my best friend and I saw something we couldn't explain, a UFO, sitting still in the air, with different colored lights swirling around in a circle. No one believed us, but we knew what we saw.

I wrote, too. Spoken word became my way of expressing myself. It made me feel alive. It made me feel heard, even when no one was really listening. I've always had a soft heart. Even as a child, I found myself loving strangers, helping where I could, feeling things deeply without always knowing why.

I used to wear leg warmers and leotards, convinced I was a dancer from the movie *Fame*. My sisters and I would all go to the neighborhood community center every Sunday and have ballet class with all our Spanish sisters. I wanted to be a dancer. I had big dreams in a small world, and I didn't mind. I had pet fish once. When I ran out of fish food, I fed them bread, not knowing any better. They immediately didn't make it lol. I remember feeling confused more than anything. I didn't understand how something so small could go so wrong.

I was afraid to sleep if my closet door was open. I owned the 4-wheel roller skates but wasn't very good at skating. Mommy used to drop me, my siblings, and cousins off at Hagy's Skating Rink almost every Friday or Saturday night, and it seemed like kids from all the neighborhoods were there.

I got my first pair of glasses at nine years old, the big, thick kind we used to call "welfare glasses." I hated them. My brothers teased me, and I wrote a storybook about it with stick figure drawings, trying to make sense of how something meant to help me made me feel so different. That was my first book with pages stapled together.

I remember getting in trouble for changing out of the shoes my mother made me wear into my favorite ones on the way to the bus stop. I thought I was being slick, changing them on the porch, but she saw me. I once set my hair on fire, being in my mom's bedroom, playing with her lighter in the dark, flicking the lighter off and on just to see what it looked like, and I had a bang at the time. I looked so crazy patting my head so hard to put the fire out. All I could think to do was grease my scalp and plait my hair up, including

what little bang I had left, so my mom wouldn't notice.

In fifth grade, I would do my schoolwork a day early

because my social studies teacher, Mr. Hawkins, would

always write the assignment for the following day on the

board. I loved science class. It made sense to me. It was the

one place where answers felt clear. I loved music and

understood and wrote it, the actual symbols. I would make

up songs using the musical notes and sing them. I loved

listening to all music, from classical to jazz to opera, reggae,

hip hop, Spanish, and even country.

I had my first boyfriend in the second grade at Foose

Elementary. His name was Charles. He had a little afro with

dimples, and his fronts were out. We used to hold hands

under the table and smile at each other. My first physical

fight was with a neighbor who was also my friend. I can't

remember her name, but she had long, red, stringy hair with

freckles all over her face. I remember running to my siblings in tears, telling them she wasn't being very nice. They encouraged me to stand up for myself, and I did, but not in the way they probably expected. I pushed her shoulder with my finger. She ran home crying, and so did I. I didn't like how it felt to fight. It didn't sit right with me. By the next day, we were back to being friends, just like that lol.

One Christmas, I tried to help my Mom open a huge, heavy cardboard box and ended up with a three-inch staple going straight through my thumb. My mother cried harder than I did. I kept telling her, "I'm okay, Mommy, it doesn't even hurt," and in that moment, it really didn't because my whole thumb was numb lol. My older brother pulled it out, and somehow, I just laughed through it (trying to make my mother feel better), but I cried immediately after. The numbness wore off.

Saturday mornings were a race. Whoever woke up first controlled the TV. My brothers usually won. I would cry until something I liked was put on or their friends came to get them to go outside. My Mom worked two jobs, and when she went to her night job, my siblings had house parties, and I learned how to do the Michael Jackson dance, "The Rock", moving my skinny little 9-year-old hips side-to-side. Those sneaky parties didn't last long because of the nosy old lady neighbors, Ms. China and Ms. Ethel told mommy. They all had to line up for a whoopin' except me. I gave my life to the Lord at the age of 17.

Those were my days. Simple, full, imperfect, and enough. I just wanted you to know a little bit about me, who I was before life asked more of me than I knew how to give.

Chapter 3

Learning Love the Hard Way

"Above all else, guard your heart, for everything you do flows from it."— Proverbs 4:23

Somewhere between the girl I used to be and the woman I was becoming, life started to change.

I stepped into adulthood carrying everything I had learned as a child, my strength, my softness, my forgiving heart, and I believed those things would be enough to guide me through life. I believed love would feel safe. I believed that if I gave my whole heart, I would receive the same in return.

But life has a way of teaching lessons that you don't see coming.

I loved deeply. That was never something I struggled with. I saw the good in people, even when it wasn't clear. I held onto hope, even when it was slipping through my fingers. And when I believed someone was meant to be in my life, I gave them deeper parts of my heart that I didn't realize were sacred. I thought I had found forever more than once.

But what I didn't understand at the time was that love should not come with fear. It should not come with confusion, pain, or the constant feeling of having to prove your worth. I didn't always recognize the difference between love and attachment, between patience and endurance, between forgiveness and self-abandonment.

And so, I stayed longer than I should have. I forgave more than I should have. I carried things that were never mine to carry. But even in that, life was not without its greatest gift—you.

Becoming a mother changed me in ways I cannot fully put into words. It gave my life a deeper purpose. It gave my heart something to fight for, something to protect, something to love beyond myself. You became my reason to keep going, even when I felt like I had nothing left to give.

As a young mom, I didn't have it all figured out. I was still learning, still growing, still hurting, still healing, still trying to understand myself while raising you. There were moments I questioned whether I was enough, whether I was doing things the right way, whether I was giving you everything you needed. But one thing I never questioned was my love for you.

Even in my hardest seasons, even when I felt lost, even when life didn't look the way I thought it would, I showed up. Maybe not perfectly, but wholeheartedly.

I began to realize that strength isn't just about what you can endure. Sometimes, strength is about what you choose to walk away from. Sometimes it's about learning to see yourself clearly, to value yourself, to understand that your heart deserves to be protected, too.

That lesson didn't come easy for me. It came through tough experience. Through heartbreak. Through moments where I had to sit with myself and ask hard questions about what I believed I deserved.

And through it all, God was there, even when I didn't fully understand Him yet. Even when my faith felt like it was still forming, still growing, still trying to find its footing.

Looking back, I can see that every step, every mistake, every moment of love and loss was shaping me into the woman I was becoming. Not perfect. Not without scars. But still standing. Still loving. Still learning.

And most importantly, still here for you.

Chapter 4

What I Carried in Silence

"Come to me, all you who are weary and burdened, and I will give you rest."— Matthew 11:28

Marriage was something I once believed would bring stability, partnership, and a sense of being covered in a way I had longed for. I thought it would be a place where love felt safe, where I could finally exhale and not have to carry everything on my own. But instead, I found myself carrying more. There were things I endured that I didn't speak about. Not because I didn't feel them, but because I was trying to hold everything together.

There were countless times I was raped and physically abused. I still carry the scars on my body. There were moments I took the beatings just to protect you, because he had become too comfortable putting his hands on you. I would say I was the one who made him angry, just to keep the focus on me.

The abuse wasn't just physical. It was emotional. Verbal. Constant. I was called names, torn down, and made to feel like no one would ever want me because of how I looked and because I had children. That's what I was told. And still…I stayed.

While we were married, he lived a double life. There were days he was gone, and I didn't know where he was. I found out he had a girlfriend and, eventually, a child with her. I didn't find out in a conversation. I found out when he brought the baby into our home. He didn't know what to do. He said she had tried to take her own life, and he took the baby and ran.

And in that moment, I didn't know what to do either. All I knew was I was tired. Tired of the phone calls where she would hang up as soon as I answered. Tired of the confusion. Tired of trying to make sense of something that didn't make sense. So, I said we could keep the baby. Raise her with you. Looking back, I realize how much I was trying to hold together something that was already broken. There was a day she showed up at our home. He acted like it was nothing. Like it didn't matter. But you had already told me that you had seen her in our house, in my bedroom, with him. He called you liars. Said you didn't know what you were talking about.

But I knew.

And I went to her house, and I fought her. Not because that was who I was, but because I was hurt, overwhelmed, and trying to release something I didn't have words for. Inside the home, things were just as heavy. His brother, who was addicted to crack and alcohol, lived with us. Rent money would be withdrawn from our shared bank account to feed his habit, and I found myself borrowing from my mother just to keep a roof over our heads.

That same brother encouraged him to leave us. To go be with his mistress and their child. I remember one night going to look for him. I found his car parked near her home. As I searched for him, his brother approached me, became physically abusive, and told me to go home. And I did.

Because at home, there was still responsibility waiting for me. A child who had just come home from spending months in a hospital, from having a brain tumor. His father, who was suffering from alcoholism and dementia, had been brought into our home because no one else wanted to care for him, even with having 14 siblings, one of whom was my age. I had to take care of this man who couldn't walk, couldn't speak, and depended on me for everything.
I fed him.
Cleaned him after releasing both ways on himself.

Bathed him.

Cut his hair.

Shaved his face.

At his funeral, his siblings and other family members would thank him and his brother for taking care of their dad, and they let them. I didn't speak because I was always seen as the 'trifling light-skinned girl', which was what I was called to my face after an introduction to his mom. Those words stayed with me, shaping how unseen I felt in that environment. His mother and siblings all treated me less than.

While raising you, going to school, working, and trying to survive emotionally, I was still dealing with a husband who was living with another woman and their child. There were times when he would come home after a conflict with her, and I became the target of what he brought back.

There were moments I had to leave you alone just so I could go to school or work, because I couldn't trust anyone to watch you. Every babysitter, as young as 18 or of a different race, he crossed boundaries with. This went on for years. Fifteen years.

We were never legally separated. Never divorced during that time. I stayed, partly out of fear, and partly because I didn't know any better. I believed that if I, as a woman, filed for divorce, I would be going against God. That belief kept me bound longer than I should have been.

Eventually, he left. Not for us, but for another woman. And then he filed for divorce, trying to make it look like it was on his terms. But my lawyer countered it on the grounds of abandonment, because that's what it was. He abandoned us after cleaning out our joint bank account. Every penny. After that, I tried to rebuild. I moved us to another state, hoping for a fresh start.

During that time, he had fallen over $2,000 behind in child support and reached out to me, saying authorities were threatening jail time. He asked if we could reach an agreement in which he would pay $250 a month, saying that was all he could afford for three children and that it would help him avoid going to jail. He promised that if I ever needed anything beyond that, he would be there to help.

I agreed. At the time, I thought I was doing the right thing, being understanding, trying to keep the peace. But he didn't keep that promise. The extra help never came. Looking back, I didn't know any better then, but I knew it hurt. I stayed single for a while. I poured myself into writing. Poetry became my outlet, something I had loved since I was younger, something I had inherited from my grandmother. It was how I released pressure and searched for peace. Performing on stage, I met someone. I thought he understood me. But he was worse.

A manipulator. A scammer. A man who lived off deception. He was selfish. He cheated constantly, exposed me to things I never should have experienced, and avoided responsibility at every turn. I worked multiple jobs, sometimes three, while pregnant with twins. He did everything he could to avoid working. Smoking weed was his pastime. He pawned the things I worked hard for. I never knew what a pawn shop was. Switched price tags in stores. Took money from charity jars. He left us homeless, living in run-down motels. He got me arrested twice.

The first time we got pulled over, he had my ID. We were already arguing, and out of spite, when the officer asked to see our IDs, he acted like he didn't have mine. He knew exactly how to push me, and the argument escalated fast. Because of my yelling at him to give up my license, I ended up in handcuffs, being taken away, while he stood there smiling. They towed the car and let him go. From across the street, he pulled my license out of his top pocket and flashed it at me, middle fingers raised, then went home as if nothing had happened.

The second time, he convinced me to write a check from a closed account, promising he would fix it immediately. I believed him. I did it. And I paid for it, with probation and another night in jail. It was a pattern for him, a history of writing bad checks. One I didn't know about until it was too late, while in court, and the Judge called him out on it. To others, he made it seem like I was the problem. Like he was just trying to build a family. But in truth, he was looking for stability, a place to stay, and he used me to get it. Even his own mother told me he preyed on other women with children and me.

I tried to protect you. I tried to keep him out when I saw what he was capable of. He even attempted to misuse my son's identity when they once shared the same name, and I had to put protections in place to stop it. Prior to that, I still tried to make things work. I opened a barbershop with my income tax money, which had a small apartment in the back. We worked there. Lived there. Tried to build something. But it still wasn't enough.

He told me I had to pay him a booth rent to work in the barbershop. Rent for the space I was already providing, labeling it "I had to pay for where I lay my head," is what he told me. Then he disappeared again. Letting other women drive the car I worked for.

Making promises about a home for all of us, showing us places, assigning rooms, only for it to never come to pass. Instead, he moved on again. Another girl who was a stripper, the same age as my daughter at the time, had two kids by her, but claimed a child who isn't biologically his. More children. More lies. I tried to shield you from it all. Not to keep you away from them, but to protect your hearts.

As you got older, you began to see things for yourselves. I could no longer shield you from the truth of who he was. And I had to carry the reality that even though those men were no longer in my life, the impact of them still lived on…in you.

Even after we broke up, the responsibility never became equal. He was originally ordered to pay $200 a month starting when you were three, but that only lasted about a year. After that, he somehow got it reduced to just one dollar a month, and it stayed that way until you turned eighteen. I fought the child support authorities, but they told me he wasn't behind and that as long as he paid something, there was nothing they could do.

So, I carried it. All of it. The separation didn't end the weight. It only made it clearer who had been carrying it all along.

This chapter is not about everything that happened. It's about what I carried through it. The silence. The endurance. The weight of trying to protect you while losing pieces of myself.

My last attempt at happiness. I believed with everything in me that I had finally chosen differently. I thought choosing someone familiar, someone connected to what I knew, would mean safety, understanding, and peace. I thought that kind of connection would protect us. What I didn't see at the time was that he used that sense of connection as a disguise. Beneath it, when I stood up to his ignorance about you, he became physically abusive. He was deceptive and destructive in ways I couldn't recognize at first. A pattern I hadn't yet broken.

Later, I came to understand that this wasn't new for him. He had a pattern of harming people, especially those who trusted him most. There are moments I still wrestle with blaming myself for choosing him when I think about how it affected you. I carry a deep sorrow knowing you were hurt in that environment. That is a weight I will always hold.

My love for you never wavered. If anything, it grew stronger. You were always the reason I kept going, even when I didn't know how I would make it through.

Chapter 5

When I Chose Me

"Forget the former things; do not dwell on the past. See, I am doing a new thing!" — Isaiah 43:18–19

There comes a moment, quiet, almost unnoticeable at first, when something inside you begins to shift. It doesn't happen all at once. Healing isn't a single moment. It's a process…a quiet unfolding.

At first, it's just a feeling. Something isn't right. Then it becomes awareness. You start noticing what you've been carrying. What you've been tolerating. What you've been losing. And then one day, you realize you've lost pieces of yourself.

Not all at once.

But little by little.

In the silence.

In the sacrifice.

In choosing everyone else.

Until one day, you look up and barely recognize the woman you've become. And that's where it begins. Not the breaking…but the rebuilding. And in that space, there was something else. There was peace. A quiet kind of peace that didn't come from everything being perfect, but from knowing I was no longer ignoring what my heart had been trying to tell me for so long.

And in that peace, I started finding myself again in the simplest ways. It didn't take much. Sometimes it was getting a cup of coffee from Wawa and sitting in my car with no rush, no expectations, no one needing anything from me in that moment.

Sometimes it was taking a drive with no destination… just moving, just breathing, just being.

Other times, it was being at home with a glass of wine, gospel music playing, and allowing myself to feel joy again. Dancing around the house, letting go, reconnecting with a part of me that had been quiet for so long. There were days I took myself out to eat. Just me. And those moments, no matter how small they may have looked to anyone else, felt big to me. Because they brought me peace.

They reminded me that I existed outside of survival. That I deserved to experience life, not just carry it. It never took much to satisfy me. But for the first time…I allowed that to be enough.

This was the beginning of rebuilding. Learning who I was again, outside of survival, outside of struggle, outside of trying to make things work that were never meant to.

I started leaning into my faith in a way I hadn't before. Not just believing in God but trusting Him. Trusting that even though I couldn't see the full picture, He was guiding me toward something better, something healthier, something whole.

I had to unlearn a lot. The idea that love meant sacrifice at the expense of myself. The belief that being strong meant enduring everything. The habit of putting my needs last without question. And in that process, I began to find myself again.

Not the version of me shaped by pain, but the version of me that had always been there, strong, yes, but also worthy of peace. Loving, but also deserving of love that feels safe.

There were still hard days. Days when I questioned, when I felt the weight of everything I had been through. But those days no longer defined me. They became part of my story, not the end of it.

Choosing myself didn't mean I stopped loving others. It meant I finally included myself in that love. And that changed everything. I was still a mother. Still present. Still committed. But now, I was also healing. Growing. Becoming.

This chapter is not about leaving something behind. It's about stepping into something new. A new mindset. A new level of faith. A new understanding of love. And for the first time in a long time, I wasn't just surviving. I was becoming.

Chapter 6

Loving You From Here

"Let all that you do be done in love." — 1 Corinthians 16:14

There is a different kind of love that comes when your children become adults. It's no longer about holding hands while crossing the street or making sure homework is done. It becomes something quieter, something more complex. A love that learns how to step back, even when your heart still wants to step in. I didn't realize how much this season would stretch me.

As you grew into your own lives, your own thoughts, your own decisions, I found myself in a place I wasn't fully prepared for. Not because I didn't want you to grow, but because I didn't expect the distance that sometimes came with it. The misunderstandings. The way my love could be seen differently through your eyes than it was through mine.

It's a different kind of hurt. Not loud. Not obvious. But quiet. Subtle. The kind that settles in your heart when you hear things about yourself that don't match the life you know you lived. When your sacrifices go unseen, or your intentions are misunderstood.

In those moments, I've had to pause. Not to defend myself. Not to argue or prove anything. But to reflect. To pray. To ask God to help me respond with love, even when I feel hurt. Because I've learned something in this season: love doesn't always mean closeness. Sometimes, love means space.

I've had to learn how to love you from where you are, not from where I wish we could be. And maybe that's why the moments we share now mean so much to me. Why sitting down for meals, whether it's all of us together or just one-on-one, fills something deeper in me than just the moment itself.

A time when those moments didn't look like this. So now, I hold onto them differently. When we're together, I take pictures. Not just to capture the moment, but to keep it. To build a memory bank I can return to, something I didn't always have the chance to do before.

Those pictures…those meals…those small moments… they mean more than they may seem. They feed something in me. They bring peace to places in my past…and quiet to parts of my future.

I don't expect you to fully understand it.

But I understand it.

And that is enough for me.

I've had to accept that your experiences, your perspectives, and your feelings are your own, even when they don't fully include or understand mine. That hasn't been easy.

There are moments I've wanted to explain everything. To walk you through every sacrifice, every decision, every silent battle I fought so you could have what you needed. But I've come to realize that not everything has to be explained to be true. God sees what was unseen. He knows what was carried in silence. And that has had to be enough for me as well.

In this season, I've also learned the importance of boundaries. Not walls, but boundaries. There is a difference. Boundaries are not about shutting you out. They are about protecting what God is healing in me. They are about choosing peace, even when emotions run deep. They are about understanding that I can love you fully without losing myself in the process. I no longer respond from a place of hurt. I respond from a place of healing, even while I'm still in the process of it. That means sometimes I am quiet. Sometimes I step back.

Sometimes I choose peace over being misunderstood. Not because I don't care, but because I care enough not to let pain define how I love you. My love for you has not changed. It has simply matured. It is no longer tied to how often we talk or don't talk, how much we agree or disagree, or how well we understand or misunderstand each other. It is deeper than that. Steadier than that. Rooted in something that life cannot shake.

And even now, I pray for you. I pray that life is kind to you. That wisdom meets you where you are. That grace finds you in moments you don't expect. And maybe one day, understanding will come, not forced, not rushed, but in its own time. Until then, I will be here.

Loving you.

Praying for you.

Respecting who you are becoming.

And trusting God with the rest.

Chapter 7

Who I Am Now

"Therefore, if anyone is in Christ, the new creation has come: The old has gone, the new is here!" — 2 Corinthians 5:17

There was a time in my life when I defined myself by what I had been through. The struggles. The relationships. The sacrifices. The survival. And while those things shaped me, they are no longer the measure of who I am. I am not just the woman who endured. I am not just the mother who sacrificed. I am not just the person who held everything together when life tried to pull it apart. I am more than that. I am a woman who has healed in places she once thought would always hurt.

A woman who has learned that strength is not just in (enduring), but in releasing. A woman who has found peace, not because life became easy, but because I stopped fighting myself. I have learned to sit with my past without living in it. To acknowledge what was, without letting it define what is.

There is a quiet confidence in me now. Not loud, not needing validation, not needing to prove anything. Just a knowing. A knowing that I did the best I could with what I had. A knowing that my love was real, even when it wasn't always received the way I hoped. A knowing that God saw every unseen moment, every silent sacrifice, every tear that no one else noticed. And that matters.

I no longer carry the weight of needing to be understood by everyone. I no longer feel the need to explain my story in a way that convinces others of my truth. My peace is no longer dependent on that. I have forgiven, not just others, but myself. For the times I stayed too long. For the times I gave too much. For the times I didn't see what I deserved sooner. Forgiveness has given me freedom.

Freedom to live without resentment. Freedom to love without fear. Freedom to move forward without constantly looking back. I still love deeply. That part of me never left. But now, my love includes me. My care includes me. My grace includes me. And that has made all the difference.

I have grown into a version of myself that I am still getting to know, but I like her. I am peaceful. I am grounded. I no longer search for myself in other people. I found myself within. And more importantly, I found God in a way that is real, not just something I heard about, but something I lived.

I trust Him now. Not just when things made sense, but even when they didn't. I trust that every part of my journey had purpose. Even the pain. Even the confusion. Even the seasons that felt like they would never end. Because they led me here. To a place of peace. To a place of clarity. To a place where I can finally say, I am whole. Not because everything in my life was perfect. But because I am no

longer broken by it.

Amber, Ashley, Angel, Seven, Khori…

If you've made it to the end of these pages, then you've read my heart. Not perfectly, not completely, but honestly.

There are things you may not have known. Things I carried quietly. Choices I made while trying to do the best I could with what I had at the time.

But through it all, one thing has never changed, my unconditional love for you.

It has never been dependent on what you say, what you believe, or how you see me. It has never required agreement or understanding. It simply is.

You were my reason in seasons when I felt like I had none. You were my strength when I felt weak. And even now, you are still a part of me in a way that life can never undo.

I release the need to be understood. I release the need to be validated. And I hold onto what matters most, love, growth, and faith.

My prayer for you remains the same:
That God guides you, protects you, and fills your life with peace. That one day, understanding meets grace. And that no matter where life takes you, you never forget how deeply you are loved. You will always be the best part of my story.

—Mom

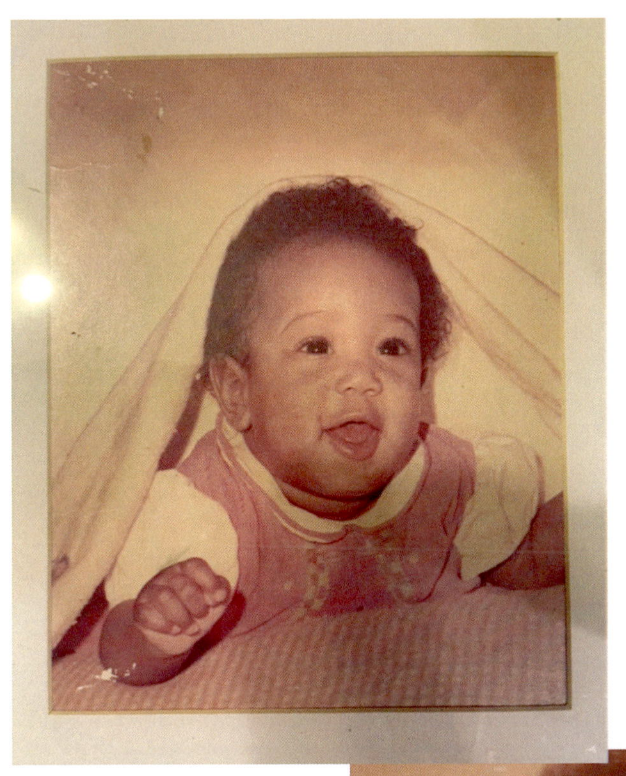

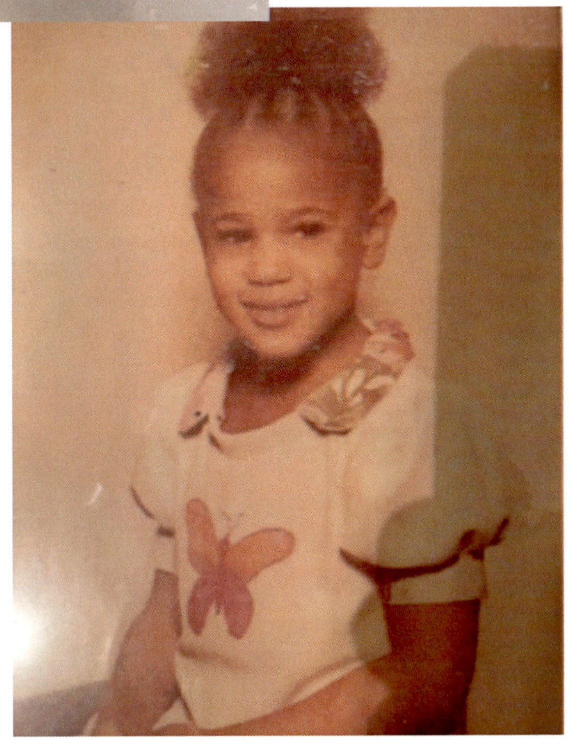